Strands of Eternity

Strands of
Eternity

A compilation
of mystical poetry and
discourses by

Vasant Lad

The
Ayurvedic
Press

Albuquerque, New Mexico

The Ayurvedic Press, Albuquerque 87112
Copyright © **2004** by Vasant Lad

This book is printed on acid-free paper.
Edited by Danielle Dorman.
Cover painting by Mary Lambert, based on a drawing by Vasant Lad.
Cover design by Michael Quanci.
Layout design by Laura Humphreys.

Printed in Thailand.
10   9   8   7   6   5   4   3   2

Library of Congress Cataloging-in-Publication Data

Lad, Vasant, 1943-
  Strands of eternity / Vasant Lad.
     p. cm.
  ISBN 1-883725-10-0 (alk. paper)
  1. Vedic poetry. I. Title.

PS3612.A355S73 2004
811'.6--dc22
                                        2004009791

Dedication

॥ श्री: ॥

This book is dedicated with all my
heart to my loving wife, Usha, who
has inspired and supported me in all
walks of my life.

by Vasant Lad

Strands of Eternity

"The Sanskrit word *Sutra*
means thread or suture.
It is as if the lower self is one piece
and the higher Self is another;
The flow of eternity sews
these two together."

The World

Within the dream of this world,
there is always the possibility of awakening.
In the drama of the dream, you are the actor,
the director, the producer.
In the dream you are many characters,
but when you wake up, the many
merge back into one.

The same is true with
your spiritual awakening.
Each person creates his own drama.
You create your own universe out of desire.

To identify yourself
with the objects of your experience
is the beginning of *unmad* – psychosis.
Objects come and go. Experiences come and go.
There is no permanence to them.

This world is a drama, a play.
Therefore, identify with this world
as an actor would identify with his role.

You play countless roles.
But you are not a beggar. You are not a king.
You talk and people laugh. You talk and people cry.
In this mad world, it is okay to act like a madman.
Act like a madman,
but keep the fire of truth
burning in your heart.

Do not forget.
It is all a play.
Die to the past. Die to this dream.
Do not get too absorbed in the drama.
Do not forget yourself.

The Witness

Let your *eyes see the objects* of this world.
Let your ears hear the sounds of this world.
While seeing and hearing,
become aware of your body.
Even while talking, walking, sitting, seeing, hearing –
witness the movement of your body.

Witness what your mind is feeling.
Notice your judgments about your feelings.
Mind and thoughts rush like a thick storm.

But you are not that thought.
You are not the fear.
You are that vast space.
Thought and fear live within you.
You are that *sakshi*, the witnessing awareness.

Thoughts come and go, like passing clouds.
Treat them as uninvited guests
and continue to witness
the movement of your mind.

Behind the movement of thought
exists your pure Self – *Asmita* –
you know it as the feeling, "I am." or "I exist."
Become one with this witnessing awareness
and jump into the inner abyss.

Look into the world
but don't choose what to look at.
Simply look. And as you look, listen.
This is *samadrishti* –
to look at things with empty eyes...
without judgment, without conclusion.

At the same time you are looking outside,
look inside your own heart.
The eyes are looking outside
but you are looking inside.
This is double-arrowed attention.

When you look at an object with empty eyes,
with no mind to choose,
suddenly the distance between you
and the object disappears.

There is no need to go on seeking.
Do not even leave your room.
Do not leave the consciousness of the witness.
In that looking, tears come to the eyes,
and you become the object you behold.

Oneness flowers and all of creation comes near.
You receive the benediction.
Though it is not the season,
flowers bloom as you pass.
Though it is not the season,
birds sing as you pass.
Though it is not their custom,
people smile as you pass.

This is the meaning of the Sanskrit word, *pujya* –
to become empty,
to become anonymous.

When you remain with your silent
witnessing awareness,
your brain cells rejuvenate
and become open to all possibilities.

Dive into this inner space
and discover who you really are.
What is your original face?

Surrender

It is often said, "Surrender to God."
But what does it mean to surrender to God?
How can we surrender
to that which we do not know?
In my daily living I know my fear. I know my anger.
I know my grief and my sadness.
These are the burning realities in the life
of every human being.
It is to these daily realities that we must surrender.

Surrendering to God means surrendering
to your awareness, your consciousness,
your experience at this very moment.
And when you look into your consciousness,
what is going on?
In between you and God
there is a barrier of thoughts, feelings and emotions.
Just half an inch behind those emotions exists
the divinity of God.
But the moment you feel those emotions
you run away.

You open the Bible. You read the Gita.
The moment you have an emotional reaction
of anxiety or anger,
you try to escape the reality.
God is eager to see you
but you are hidden
behind your anger, fear and insecurity.
Surrender to what you are feeling.
This is the only way to bridge the distance between
you and God.

Surrender can't be practiced.
It happens now or never.
When you surrender to every moment,
your life becomes a celebration.
Celebrate each feeling, each thought, every emotion
and your life will flow like a river.
The river is born deep within the mountain.
It flows through the jungles and valleys,
through cities and villages
and ultimately the river merges with the ocean.

Surrender is the river that will deliver you back
to the ocean of cosmic consciousness.

Be With What Is

Life has its own momentum.
Life has its own agenda.
But the ego in its foolishness wants to control life.
What is, is!
"What is" is not static. It is ever evolving.
"Should be, would be, could be" are ideas,
which is illusion.

When you remain with what is,
there is a death of the mind.
There is a death of ego.

To love something means to accept it completely.
Give complete awareness to what is
and what is flowers
and showers benediction on you.

Look at what is with all your mind,
with all your heart
and all your gut.

Then your grief, your attachment,
your longing or your discontent
will burst into pure bliss.
This is your true nature.

This life is most unique.
Don't waste it on trifles.
Every moment, live it completely.
Everything is here.
The entire Universe is throbbing
in your heart.
The entire existence is breathing
in your lungs.

Surrender to what is
is surrender to God.
And in that surrender the door opens.
When you surrender to what is,
then what is ends.
And what remains is the transformation of a man.

No religion can give you that.
No guru can give you that.
Do you have the gut, the courage
to be with what is?

Action

Conscious action is total action.
The action done in consciousness is complete.
It is done and ended there.
Then there is action without the actor,
doing without the doer.
Doing without doer-ship is worship.
This complete action, done in awareness,
leaves no scar on the mind.

Unconscious action is incomplete action
which leaves a scar on the mind.
And total number of scars are called *samskara*,
the cause of birth and death.
Incomplete actions leave fingerprints
in the sky of consciousness.

Your every effort is the barrier
that keeps you from conscious action.
Though you must use effort,
use it only until the efforting drops
of its own accord.

Your every movement towards
the goal of enlightenment
pushes it farther away.
Your desire for enlightenment
is just another projection of the ego.

When you learn the art of acting out of nothingness,
you will no longer create *karma*.
Karma is action out of knowledge,
out of preoccupation.
When you act out of nothingness,
when you act out of complete awareness,
no scar is created on the sky of consciousness.

Desire

Desire has its root in the past memory of pleasure.
Within the womb of memory, desire is born.
Desire is the drive, the main source of action.
There is no action without desire.

There is desire in the soul to take birth as a child.
There is desire in the child to become an adult.
And there is desire in the adult to make money,
to prosper and to achieve.
Our hearts contain even a desire for God,
a desire for salvation,
a desire for ultimate bliss.
But God is not the product of desire.

Knowing this, we practice non-desire.
But practicing no desire is also desire!
Having desire to achieve,
and not having desire to achieve,
both are the internal, twin forces of desire.

Neither having desire nor denying desire
can help us in our quest for the uttermost.
Both conditions produce a glue
that binds us to our concepts.

Desire plays a very important role
in the life of every human being.
Watch your desire. Observe it. Feel it.
Do witnessing of it, and let it flower.
The flowering of desire is the ending of it.
And when desire ends, there is freedom.

When desire drops, you become the host
and God becomes the guest.
And God rushes to you from all directions.

Attachment

Attachment is the food of the mind.
Attachment is the anchor of the mind.
Through attachment the mind anchors
to many things in this world.

Such a mind is a jailed mind.
Where there is attachment there is no freedom.
Where there is attachment there is no love.
The attachment you feel to a particular outcome
is like a vehicle.
Let the vehicle take you on a journey
but when you arrive, you must leave it
outside the door
and enter the destination alone.

Some have become unhappy with attachment
so they decide to practice detachment.
This detachment is but
another face of attachment.
It is based on control.

The stem of attachment has given rise
to the sprout of detachment.
Both stems spring forth from
the root of ego.

You may have given up outer clinging.
You may practice spiritual austerities.
But have you given up the inner clinging?
The clinging to enlightenment
prevents the transformation you so desire.

You cannot force open the flower
of spiritual freedom.
It blooms on its own accord.
If you force it, it may appear to bloom.
But in reality it is already dead.

Where there is attachment, there is no awareness.
Give complete attention to your attachment.
Apply your whole body, mind and emotions to it.
A space will open
and that attachment will drop by itself
like a mature leaf drops to the ground.

Emotion

Half an inch behind your suffering
there is bliss.
Give complete attention to your grief,
to your sadness, to your anger.
Let it flower.
Don't counsel it, suppress it, analyze it.

Your grief is your reaction.
Your grief is your projection.
Suffering is within. It does not come from without.
The moment you realize the real relationship
between yourself and suffering, it ends.

Suffering comes to you to awaken you.
Use your suffering as a springboard
and dive deep within.
Be with your emotions.
You can't avoid pain by pursuing pleasure.
I do not know the name of the pleasure
which does not end in pain.

Pleasure is a poor substitute for joy.
You can invite pleasure but you cannot invite joy.
You cannot invite joy because joy is you!
Shivo 'aham, Shivo 'aham!

Look at your sadness, your anger, your jealousy.
They are but a mirror.
Look at the emotion
and look also at the looker of the emotion.

This is the meaning of *prati prasava* –
moment to moment delivery.
As you feel the emotion,
observe the movement of your consciousness
and let it pass.
Then you are born again, anew.
Out of the womb of that anger,
out of the womb of that grief.

Before the emotion can pass,
it must be thoroughly digested.
Emotions which are unripe
cloud the thinking
and block awareness.

How to ripen uncooked emotions?
Bring total awareness to the sensation.
Give yourself totally to the sadness,
to the grief, to the fear.
Ripen the emotion with the flame of awareness.

The moment you become aware
your reaction flowers
and melts into nothingness.
Swallow that hurt, digest it completely
and let it yield into pure awareness.
Emotion is reaction.
Love is total action.

Anger

Anger represents a lack of attention,
a preoccupation with past memory.
The past memory meets with the present situation
and creates a reaction.
Unprocessed experiences create an image
but enlightened people have no image.
Flattery and insults dissolve in their awareness,
just as the ocean doesn't react to being called a fool.

Offer your emotions to the flame of awareness.
Your grief was created in darkness,
in unconsciousness.
Awareness brings the past action to maturity.
Awareness is a flame that roasts the past memory.
And roasted seeds do not sprout.

Loneliness

No cloud can stain the sky.
Through identification you create
a cloud of fear, a cloud of anger.
Yet the sky of consciousness remains stainless.

You were born alone.
When you are alone, you are with God.
The moment you depart from your aloneness
you become lonely.
Then you try to move away from loneliness –
you go to the movie, you watch TV.

Loneliness is ugly. Aloneness is beautiful.
Do not fight your loneliness. Allow it to flower.
Be alone.

In the mirror of relationships
you can watch your loneliness.
At the same time I look at you,
I am looking at the center of my heart.
Then there is looking without the looker,
and listening without the listener.
You are not the looker or the listener.
You are one with the throbbing of life.

Fear

Your fear is not your fear, but that of all mankind.
Meditate upon fear.
The fear response becomes habitual –
an unconscious, mechanical rushing act.
Allow your awareness to move with the fear.
Let your awareness go with the movement.

Pay attention as you walk,
as you listen, as you speak.
Each time the fear comes as a rushing automatic act,
let it move slower.
See the gap between two fears,
then fear yields into awareness itself.

I have heard some students say,
"This is hard to do."
It is neither hard nor easy.
It simply is.
Learn to love your fear.
Learning is not judging or accumulating.
Learning is unlearning. It is loving.

Judgment

Judgment is fragmentation.
When judgment comes, let it come.
Let it pack but don't let it store.
Breathe deeply all the while.

Don't keep chewing on the judgment,
like a dog chews a dry bone.
The dog keeps on chewing and chewing,
though there is no juice there.
Soon the dog's own gums start to bleed
and the dog believes the juice
has come from the bone.

The bone is bleeding the dog,
and the judgment bleeds the judge.

When judgment comes, don't suppress it.
Judge it.
End it there and walk.

Even to say that a flower is beautiful
means that there is no communion
between you and that flower.
Let go of the judgment and become the beauty.
You are that beauty.

Withdraw your attention from the object
and look at the subject.
Then subject becomes object
and you jump into the witnessing awareness.

Just half an inch behind your judgment
there is a God waiting for you.
The confused mind judges
between ugliness and beauty.
The clear mind sees no difference.

Beauty and ugly are the same,
just as love is not the opposite of hate.
Who is the one making the judgment?
Go to that source.

You are not the beautiful, you are the beauty.
You are not loving anyone, you are the love.
You are not looking for the light, you are the light.
The one who is truly religious
doesn't need to carry a flag.

The Art of Looking

Look deliberately at a tree or a flower.
Look completely, with total attention.

Thoughts will rush to judge that flower.
Take a long breath.
Return again to the looking.
See the color, the beauty,
the total existence of the flower.

The past memory will rush toward you.
But remain in the art of looking.
When there is pure observation without thought,
your mind will be like a blank screen,
clear to reflect the intelligence of the cosmos itself.
This profound intelligence is called *Mahat*.

At that moment, you fall in love with the flower.
This is unconditional love.

In the beginning, the art of looking is a practice –
conscious, deliberate.
Then it becomes your second nature.
Then you see the whole existence
without the stain of prejudice
without the barrier of the past.

You are given only one moment at a time.
Really speaking, no other moment exists.
Enjoy this moment.
Celebrate this moment.
The moment of no movement is meditation.

Reflections in a Mirror

Life is an interplay between inner and outer.
The inner is what you are.
It is your pure awareness.
The outer is the projection
of your accumulated experiences.

Your individual consciousness is but a reflection
of universal consciousness.
Through the mirror of *buddhi*, the intellect,
universal consciousness is reflected
as individual consciousness.

Life is a never-ending relationship
between inner and outer.
And relationships are a mirror.
In the mirror of your relationships
arise the reflections of your subconscious emotions.
Even a word or a gesture
can bring to the surface what was once
hidden deep within.

When you watch yourself
in the mirror of relationships,
your mind is seeing itself.
And there is nothing the mind resists more
than looking at itself!
The mind likes to look at the sunset, the flower,
or better yet, the other woman or man.

Develop the knack of looking at yourself
through the mirror of the world.
This mirror never tells a lie.
Use the mirror of relationship to discover
what lies behind its reflection.

Relationships are the school for self inquiry
into the nature of yourself.

The Flame of Awareness

Let not the flame of your awareness
be clouded by conclusion.

No book should be your Bible.
Let your daily operating awareness be your Bible.
Let your daily operating awareness be your Gita.
And your daily functioning perception
be your Koran.

Come to know the flame of awareness
that is burning in your heart.
It is a flame of love,
a flame of attention.
The action of awareness doesn't nourish ego.
The action of awareness has no shadow of fear.

Awareness is emptiness, perception,
clarity, presence.
Awareness is your true nature.

In true awareness you are not aware
that you are aware,
yet you are aware of everything.
Awareness is supreme intelligence.
It is love, freedom, beauty.

Consciousness is awareness plus intellect.
It is preoccupation, priority, pre-determination.
Consciousness is the product
of education and culture.
Consciousness is superficial.

The flame of awareness has always been with you.
No one can take it from you.
Neither can anyone can give it to you,
either in heaven or on earth.

No *guru* can give it to you.
He or she can only show the way,
like a finger pointing to the moon.
The discovery of your innermost awareness
must be made for yourself.

Consciousness is a personal phenomenon.
Awareness is impersonal, total.
You are awareness.

Knowledge from the past comes from memory.
Knowledge in the present moment
comes from *atman*, the inner being.
Emotions are a reaction.
Awareness is action.
It is spontaneous.
The action of awareness cannot be predicted
or premeditated.
It happens of its own accord.

Emotional Purification

According to Ayurveda,
the ancient science of self-knowledge,
the emotional body can be purified
by the same methods
which purify the physical body.

Srotomukha vishodhanam is cleansing the passages
through which emotions flow.
If there is fear, anxiety, anger – surrender to it.
That letting go opens the channels of circulation.
Then the emotion can move freely.

Vrudhi means to increase the impurity.
On the psychological level,
the emotions must be provoked
before they can be released.
Encourage crying, see a sad movie,
do anger release work.
This gets the emotion moving,
but doesn't end it for good.

Abhisyandhan is de-crystalization
or liquefication of emotion.
It makes the emotion as a fluid
just as salt or sugar melts in the sun.

This can be done with deep tissue work,
vigorous massage
or by reclining the body in a gentle easy posture –
this will help your emotions become liquid.

You cannot yield juice from an unripe mango.
If you try, you will destroy the mango.
Then you will have neither the mango nor its juice!
But if you ripen the mango
the juice flows easily from the fruit.
This ripening is called *pachan*,
which digests the emotion and brings maturation.
Maturity is the perfume of life.

To ripen your emotions, bring your total awareness
to your feelings.
The memory of an insult is lodged in your mind –
bring complete awareness to it
and you will no longer be attached to it.
Stay with your grief with total awareness.

The flame of awareness will cook your grief
and like a dry leaf it drops to the ground.
Stay near your feelings. Stay near God.

Fast from food. Fast from talking.
Allow the emotion to ripen.
Allow your grief and anger to flower and they will die
their own natural death.
Suppress them and they will fight for their existence.

Deepan means to enkindle the flame of awareness.
Stay in the stops between your breath.
Stay in the gap between your thoughts.
Meditation is the medium through which
the flame of awareness is enkindled.

The Shadow

Under every lamp there is darkness.
The bigger the source of the light,
the bigger the area of darkness.

You create your own darkness.
Whatever experience occurs
which is not to the liking of your ego,
that experience is pushed away.

The ego eats the banana of pleasure
and throws away the skin of pain.
When at a later time you trip
over that banana peel,
you forget that you, yourself, left it there.
You think it was placed there by the world.

Darkness comes from within.
Light also comes from within.
What you see when you look into the world
is nothing but a projection
of your own consciousness.
You are the world and the world is you.

In the recesses of deep unconsciousness
live the things you have hidden from yourself.
In the recesses of your body's connective tissues
live the experiences you would rather forget.
Though they are not in your conscious awareness,
they are there in your shadow.

There is heaven in you
and there is also hell within you.
Heaven and hell are not geographical locations.
Heaven and hell exist inside you.

When your mind starts to project outwards
what it has denied within itself,
that is hell.

And when you have the gut to be with what is,
when your conscious awareness has shone
on the dark corners of your mind,
when your mind is clear and not resistant,
you open the door to heaven.

Darkness is what you are not conscious of.
You cannot do anything about your darkness.
You can only approach darkness
through the light of consciousness.

Pay attention to inattention.
And become conscious of your unconsciousness.
There your shadow will transform into light.

The Ego

Really speaking, there is no ego.
It is an empty shell; a shadow; a process.
Your body is made of five elements –
earth, water, fire, air and ether – where is the ego?
Ego is not a substance. It is a shadow.
A shadow of memory, a shadow of knowledge.
Watch the emptiness of the ego every moment.

Breathing is the first door of ego.
You think you are breathing your body
but what you see in the rise and fall of your breath
is the work of God.
You do not know. You are not doing it.
Respiration happens.
The moment you say, "I am breathing,"
you open the door of ego.
Desires and thoughts then enter
through your breath.

Breath comes from God, from nothingness,
not from you.
Let your breathing be a worship to *prana*,
the creative dynamic force.

When you breathe with awareness,
you allow God to breathe through you.
Close the door of ego
which enters through the breath.

Doing is the second door of ego.
The ego says, "I can do it!"
Not doing is the ending of the ego.
Not doing is meeting nothingness.

Workaholism is childish.
It enhances the concept of "me and my."
A child learns to throw a ball
and he derives self-esteem from that act.

You have become addicted to the rewards.
Now you throw the ball in order to get the reward.
The world calls this growth, achievement, fame.

While doing art, the artist is not.
Art happens.
It is the continuous spontaneous flow of intelligence.
So far, so good.

But when picture is done,
ego comes and artist signs his name.
How ridiculous!
The bird, though he flies with grace,
does not leave fingerprints in the sky.

Name is the third door of ego.
Name is the preoccupation with identity.
"My father is better than your father" or
"My *guru* is better than your *guru*."
It may be a good idea to change your name.

Merely carrying a label of religion that says,
"I belong to this or that religion,"
does not make you truly religious.
True religion has no adjective.
Adjectives are identification.
Why do you need such identification?

You are anonymous!
You are without attribute.
Nothingness is real sanity.
Running away from nothingness is insanity.
Come to rest in your nothingness.

Reasoning is the fourth door of ego.
The ego asks, "Why does it happen?
Why did you do that? I want to know!"
It is a fruitless question.
For no reasoning whatsoever can satisfy the ego.

Becoming is the fifth door of ego.
You are always seeking to become
more than you are.
You want to advance in the society.
Everyone wants to become somebody;
no one wants to become nobody!

Becoming is running away from being.
When you try to become somebody
you run away from what you already are.
The wanting after somebody-ness
is the beginning of madness.

All possibilities are there
when you remain with what you are.

Do not run after what should be,
would be, could be.
This is madness.
Be with what is.

Slip into that nothingness.
Enter into *nirvana*.
Blow out the flame of ego
and disappear into eternity.

Mind

You may think your brain is thinking.
But your thinking is not personal, it is universal.
Within the sky of consciousness,
clouds of thoughts are passing through.
You identify with those thoughts
and call them your own.

Yet they are no more yours
than the clouds in the sky.
When you identify with the thoughts,
you become the thinker.
Then you judge your thoughts.

Within the sky of consciousness,
thought clouds come and go.
Yet sky remains absolutely stainless –
pure, sacred.
Thoughts cannot stain
the sky of your consciousness.

Mind is a river of thoughts.
Like a river is the mind.
As is the water, so is the river.
If the water is clear, the river is clear.
If the water is cloudy, the river is cloudy.
If the water is abundant, the river is flooded, swollen.
As is the thought, so is the mind.
As is the mind, so is the man.

Your mind is caught in a traffic jam,
bumper to bumper with thoughts.
You identify with these thoughts,
and lose yourself in the identification.
Mind makes you sad.
Mind makes you fearful.
Mind makes you happy.
The servant has become the master.

Do not look to your thoughts for happiness.
Thoughts can never make you happy.
Just as you cannot get a tree by dissecting a seed.
Manas, or mind, means
"that which exists only on non-existent things."
The mind exists only in the past and the future.

The past has happened. It is no more.
The future has yet to happen. It does not exist.

Mind is movement.
Manas and *prana* go together.
If you sit quiet and watch the movement
of your mind
it will yield into pure perception.

As you sit quiet there will come
a death of the mind.
And you enter into a no-mind state.

Remain as a witness to your mind.
Be aware of your thoughts,
be aware of your feelings.
Suddenly the blocks will open.

Treat your mind as a dear friend.
Bring your thoughts a bunch of flowers.
When your mind races wildly
say to it:

"Oh my mind, what you have accumulated
you are now experiencing!
Oh my mind, do not get stuck with *maya*.
Your death is approaching towards you.
Do not get stuck with illusion, with pride."

"When your death attacks you,
no one can save you.
Neither your wife, nor the minister,
nor your friends can protect you.
You are dying alone.
At that moment
only your conscious awareness will protect you.
Only *so-hum*. I am That."

"Oh my mind, look how beautiful you are.
You have created a maze!
What you have accumulated,
you are now experiencing."

It doesn't matter if your mind
goes to heaven or to hell.
Do not yield an inch from your inner awareness.
Remain as a witness to the movement
of your mind.

Unless you pull the bow,
the arrow of thought cannot fly.

In the space of no mind
there is clarity, beauty.
In the space of no mind
there is God.

Meditation

Just as there is a space between
the clouds in the sky,
there is a space between your thoughts.
This space is the doorway to the divine.

If you identify yourself with your thoughts
you become the thinker.
If the thought brings fear,
you identify with that fear
and you become afraid.

But you are not that thought.
You are not that fear.
You are that vast space.
Thought and fear live in you.
When you fight with your thoughts,
you lose your energy.
Just watch the space between two thoughts.

Pay attention to inattention;
then inattention becomes attention.
Jump into the space, the inner abyss.
Clouds come and go,
yet sky remains absolutely spotless, sacred.
No thought can stain the sky of consciousness.

Breathe consciously with total awareness.
Slow down your breathing
until you can see a little space –
a gap.

That gap is most important.
Remain in that gap. It will get wider.
Dive into the space. Dive into the inner abyss.
You are so vast.
The whole Universe is within you.
The roots of heaven exist
in the silent spaces between your thoughts.
Once you are in that abyss,
"You" as an individual are absent.
You forget your thoughts,
you forget the world.

Now, at this moment, just sit quietly
and feel the presence of God around you.
Listen to the silence.

Can you hear some ringing noise in the ear?
Listen to it as it merges into silence.
Don't concentrate. But just be aware.
Pay attention.
And you will feel that expanse is taking place.

Listen to your thoughts.
Listen to your feelings, emotions.
Bring more awareness
and pay complete attention to your thinking.
You will see a gap,
a silent gap between two thoughts.

In that silence there is no mind.
The gap enhances and you become empty.
Let that inner space expand
in all directions equally.

Your breath is moving naturally.
Let the lungs do their job of breathing.

You are simply watching the breath.
It goes in and comes out.
And there is a stop behind the belly button.
Stay in that stop for a fraction of a second.

And when the lungs exhale, follow the breath.
Come back to the diaphragm, heart, trachea, nose.
During exhalation air goes out.
Follow the breath.
Go out of your body and stay in the outer stop.

These two stops, outer and inner,
are most important.
In that stop there is no mind.
There is silence, peace.
That stop is called *Rama*.

Do not do pre-meditated meditation.
Meditation should be alive, flowing like a river,
at *every* moment of your life.
Meditation creates discipline which allows you
to find your Self at *every* moment.
To reach the *jivanmukta*, the innermost core,
no system or method is needed.

Methods and systems simply prepare the ground.
They make the ground of your consciousness fertile
for the flowering of meditation.

Once the flower is blooming,
all systems and techniques automatically disappear.
Drop the system. Drop the technique.
Be aloof. Be alone.
And enter into the Self.

You cannot invite meditation,
it simply comes.
You just have to be open.

Like a breeze meditation comes to you.
The sunlight is always there,
you only need to open the door.

Do not expect anything from meditation.
Just sit casually and watch your breath,
stay in the stop.
Soon that stop will stay with you.
When you walk, God walks with you.
And you are walking in God.

Only God exists.
And God's existence is that stop.
That stop is the *jivanmukta*.
That stop is you.

The End of Knowledge

You carry a cloud of confusion,
conclusion and judgment
around the flame of your awareness.
Knowledge obstructs perception.
In truth, knowledge is ignorance.

Perception which is learned phenomenon
is knowledge.
Perception which is pure phenomenon
is intelligence.
Unless you renounce knowledge
you cannot attain intelligence.

Knowledge is so small
and existence is so vast and profound.
Perhaps due to fear you cling to knowledge.
Fear is the instrument of the ego.
Renounce the ego. Renounce knowledge.
Then the nervous system becomes pliable.

The map is not the territory.
You must be in the presence of the real sun
and the real moon in order to get light.
You cannot get light from a picture of these things.
No words can contain the mystery of life.

Knowledge is like a beautiful silk flower.
Though its petals are intricate and lifelike
it has no perfume.
Wisdom is the real flower.
It has a perfume of intelligence.

Knowledge can be gained from any book,
but wisdom must be learned from a master.
If you are open, *Buddha*,
even the dead master will come to you.
If you are closed, if you cling to knowledge,
even the living master can't get in.

You become crazy
when you carry around too much knowledge.
It is a barrier to knowing one another.
When you carry around knowledge
you look from the past,

you see the face of another from the past,
and you don't see the real being.

Knowledge can become a tool of the ego.
It is a plastic flower which creates more ego.
You spend so much time
watering this plastic flower,
but it cannot grow.

Even knowledge can become corrupt
when it operates through the ego.
Then you become the leader of a confused world.
You become the leader of a confused ashram.

Die in every moment to what you know.
Drop what you know and become knowledge itself.
Life is a mystery, not a puzzle.

Knowing is *banda*, a prison.
Not knowing is *mukti*, which is freedom.

Your intelligence, not your knowledge, will tell you
whether someone is real or pseudo.
You can understand the person by the way he looks,

by the way he moves and speaks.
There is no need of name.

Simply observe through
intuition and inner awareness.
This is *samadhi* in action.
Apply your whole awareness to an object
and gain direct knowledge of that object.
This is *samyama*.
Let your daily operating awareness be your bible.

True understanding comes
from the light which is inside.
There is no need to leave the source.
There is no need to leave the source.

Death

Your body belongs to the earth,
to the water, to the air, to the space.
The grace of the five elements
gave you your body.

You exist in your body through the process of time.
But you are not this body.
Neti, neti – not this, not this.
You are not this.

At the time of death the elements
return to their source.
First the fire element leaves
as fever burns in the dying person.
Then the person begins to perspire,
as if the water element is also returning to its source.

What remains is the last breath.
The dying person gasps for air
as the air element leaves the body.

Now you are packing.
You cannot hear; your ears are already packed.
You cannot see; your sight is already packed.
You have packed even your hands and legs
in the suitcase of your astral body.

When death comes, you take hold of
the rope of *prana*
and jump into the abyss.
What is left is just an empty earthen pot.

You do not die
because *you were* never born.
Birth and death are a dream.
You have no birth! You have no death!
You exist here for awhile.
You are like a sacred tree
whose roots are up
and whose branches are down.

Death is a returning to your original source.

Awakening

In your daily life you move freely
between three states of awareness –
deep sleep (*sushupti*), dreaming (*swapna*),
and awakening (*jag gruti*).
But though you pass through
these three stages every day,
still you are not awake.
You remain asleep to the present moment.

If today is cloudy, you go on dreaming
about yesterday's sunny skies.
If in this moment you are angry,
you wistfully remember happy times.

In every moment you have the power to awaken.
But where you have expectation, desire, or the need
to achieve a result, there can be no awakening.
Desire and expectation keep you stuck in the dream.
The vastness of your true self is no longer free,
but is chained by memory and desire.

You long to awaken from your slumber.
You yearn to understand Life as a whole
and to know your place in the universe.
So you search for a mantra, a technique, a teacher –
you think you need an outside agency
to awaken you to the truth.
But the power to awaken lies within you.

Awakening is awareness. It is mindfulness.
Bring total attention to what is happening
at this moment.
What are your eyes seeing?
What are your ears hearing?
What is your mind thinking?

Listen completely to the call of a bird,
the cry of a child,
the barking of a dog, or the rattle of a truck.
Listen to every sound that comes to you,
without liking it, disliking it or judging it.

The sound is rushing towards you to meet you.
Listen to the outer sound and let it pass through you.
Follow the sound as it dissolves
into the center of your being.

Peace is listening to the sound, not you.
When peace listens to the sound
there is no judgment.
Peace is not the opposite of sound.
Peace is the source of sound.
Peace is the original sound.
Awakening unfolds when not a single thing
is excluded from your awareness.
Outer looking and inner looking go together.
Outer doing and inner doing go together.

First you experience an outer awakening –
you become aware of the objects around you.
Then you experience a physical awakening –
you become aware of your body, your posture.
Finally you experience an inner awakening –
you awaken to your internal thoughts,
feelings and emotions.
And from there you can jump into awareness itself.
Your consciousness expands and you awaken
to the whole world,
the whole galaxy, the whole solar system.
The entire Universe unfolds from within you.

To be awake is to see Life as a whole.
You must be awake to see the dawn of love.
You must be awake to perceive the dawn of light.
Unless you are awake, you cannot hear
the whisper of God.

Enlightenment

Your heart is a womb
that longs to become pregnant with God.
When a woman is pregnant she is so content.
She does not look outside to the other man.
She is so content.
She just looks down and smiles.
She is so fulfilled.

Become pregnant with God.
Do not look outside yourself.
No one can enlighten you.
Even the *guru* is just a mirror.

Enlightenment is not the product of want.
Enlightenment is not the product of desire.
If you meditate to become enlightened,
it will take a very long time.
You must surrender even to the desire
to become enlightened!

Enlightenment is now or never.
It is at every moment.
It is not tomorrow, not next lifetime.
It is now, at this very moment.

One glance of perception opens the door to heaven.
God is beating in your heart.
God is breathing in your lungs.
God is feeling through your mind.

God is working in your body at every moment,
but you are not aware.
Who digests your food?
Who creates new cells?
Who heals your wounds?
You and God are inseparable.

When you attain the highest state of enlightenment,
the world becomes your mirror.
The distinction between inner and outer
disappears.

When you become enlightened,
the whole of existence becomes happy.

The Journey

During meditation,
when the breath settles,
when the mind settles,
one feels small like an atom
and huge like outer space.
The drop becomes the ocean
and the ocean becomes the drop.

One has the feeling of lightness
and one's desires are fulfilled without asking,
without manipulating.

People begin talking about such a person,
and he becomes famous
among people, birds, plants and animals.
He feels intense devotion towards God,
as if God is both the lover and the beloved.

His consciousness becomes so expansive,
that eventually he remembers his true nature
at every moment of his life.

Do not worry if along your spiritual journey
people begin talking about you,
feeling jealous of you, and lying about you.
This is a very good sign.
It means you are gaining spiritual energy.
And their criticism will help you to burn the ego.

The journey has begun.

The Otherness

As you sit silently observing the objects of this world
suddenly the Otherness comes.
It is so tactile you can touch it.
It is palpable.

It comes like a breeze.
It comes from the cloud.
It comes like a familiar song.
It comes when you do not expect it.
It comes suddenly.
Sometimes it comes from within you.

When the Otherness comes,
it brings with it the void.
You have spent your whole life
running from the void.
There is no need to be afraid.
You are the Otherness
and the Otherness is God.
You and that Otherness are one.

The Otherness is the expression
of the totality of existence.
The Otherness welcomes you.
The Otherness hugs you.
But will you be there to receive it?

When the Otherness comes
there is no mind, no thought.
You can feel it, touch it, experience it,
but you cannot describe it.

Don't even try.
The Otherness will speak through your mouth.
It is there. You have only to receive it.
Become a receptionist.

It is speaking.
It is listening.
But still it is alone.
It doesn't belong to you,
but you are That.

"Aham Brahmasmi" means in Sanskrit,
"I am the Universe."
This is not a declaration
nor an announcement.
But an innermost experience.

The One Behind
the Many

You are seeking the One that is behind the many.
If you don't understand the One, the unity,
you cannot understand the many, the multiplicity.
You were born whole and complete,
but you have become fragmented.

Though you are free
you are caught in the prison
of identification and justification.
You seek your whole life
for that which you already are.
This is the ultimate irony.

You are seeking that which you originally are.
When a child is born, a seeker is born.
Wake up!

When you dream you become many,
but the moment you wake from the dream
the many merge back into one.
In the same way, this world is filled
with countless faces and forms.
But when you wake up,
all you see is the one behind them all.

Dreams are many but the dreamer is one.
Objects are many but the observer is one.
You are always trying to meet the one.

The sun is one
though it is reflected in many pots.
There is always duality in reality.
There are many realities in this world,
but truth is one.

Other Books by Vasant Lad

Ayurveda: The Science of Self-Healing. 1985
Secrets of the Pulse: The Ancient Art
of Ayurvedic Pulse Diagnosis. 1996
The Complete Book of Ayurvedic Home Remedies.
1998
The Textbook of Ayurveda: Fundamental Principles.
Volume One. 2002

The Yoga of Herbs: An Ayurvedic Guide
to Herbal Medicine. 1986
by Vasant Lad and David Frawley

Ayurvedic Cooking for Self-Healing. 2nd ed., 1997
by Usha and Vasant Lad

Coming Soon

The Textbook of Ayurveda: A Complete Guide to
Clinical Assessment. Volume Two. 2005
by Vasant Lad
Marma Points of Ayurveda: The Energy Pathways for
Healing Body, Mind and Consciousness. 2005
by Vasant Lad and Anisha Tambay